Vexed

Vexed

Elizabeth Poreba

RESOURCE *Publications* · Eugene, Oregon

VEXED

Copyright © 2015 Elizabeth Poreba. All rights reserved. Except for brief quotations in critical publications or reviews, no part of this book may be reproduced in any manner without prior written permission from the publisher. Write: Permissions. Wipf and Stock Publishers, 199 W. 8th Ave., Suite 3, Eugene, OR 97401.

Resource Publications
An Imprint of Wipf and Stock Publishers
199 W. 8th Ave., Suite 3
Eugene, OR 97401

www.wipfandstock.com

ISBN 13: 978-1-4982-1888-7

Manufactured in the U.S.A. 05/13/2015

"Village Church," "One-Sided Dialogue Concerning the Soul" and "Jonah" appeared previously in *Commonweal*.

"The Career of That Enigmatic Man" appeared in *Spiritofstbarts* (online)

"Iris" and "St. Kateri" appeared in *First Literary Review East* (online)

Scriptural passages from the Holy Bible, New International Version®, NIV®. Copyright © 1973, 1978, 1984, 2011 by Biblica, Inc.™ Used by permission of Zondervan. All rights reserved worldwide. www.zondervan.com The "NIV" and "New International Version" are trademarks registered in the United States Patent and Trademark Office by Biblica, Inc.™

Cover Image: John Mann, Untitled, from *Drift*, 2013

Members of the O'Clock Poets—Maura Candela, Guillermo Castro, John Couturier, Ron Drummond, Katie Johntz, Amy Lemmon, Katrinka Moore, Martie Palar, Joan Poole, Sarah Stern—read and pondered most of these poems with me, and I can never thank them enough.

for all the saints, known and unknown

Contents

Off Balance

Vexed 2
Why, my soul, are you downcast? 3
Mystery 4
Cryptic 5
Abraham and Sarah
Get the Unlikely News 6
Of the Career of That
Enigmatic Man, 7
St. Joseph's Church,
Stephentown, New York 8
Martin Burnham, 1959–2002 9
Village Church 10
The Winchester Bible 11
Wild Carrot 12
Hypocrite 13
Why Should We Think 14
Jonah 15
Ascension Thursday 16
Feast of the Immaculate Conception 17

Surrounding Field

Accounts 21
Inheritance 22
The Heathen School in Cornwall,
Connecticut, 1817–1826 23
Pewter 24
Tax Time 25
The Visit 27
Repair 28
Particular 29
Love and Do What You Will 30
Manna 32
Warmth 33

CONTENTS

Angles of Repose

Three Saints	37
The Famous Ecstasy	38
St. Teresa Wrote	40
One-Sided Dialogue Concerning the Soul	41
Annunciation	42
Feast of the Assumption	43
Possible Saint	44
St. Lucy	45
Feast of the Transfiguration, August 6	46
Iris	47
Vespers	48
Crèche	49
(1)	50
(2)	51
(3)	52
(4)	53
(5)	53
(6)	53
St. Kateri Tekakwitha	54
Piety	55
The Rosary	56
Former Doves	58
Ritual	59
The Apple Tree	60
Shadrach, Meshach, and Abednego	61
Forecast	62
He makes his wind blow and the waters flow	63
Faith	64
Let all the trees of the forest sing for joy	65
So, My Saints	66
Notes	67

Off Balance

Vexed

Why not speak of it
made of rays

A large presence
that does not press upon us

Why not people the blue
populate the waste space

Set the table
arrange the cup and plate

Mark the calendar
to the end of time

Smooth back
the title page

Address this vexed topic
neither wave

Nor particle

Why, my soul, are you downcast?

It's living with that old lady, isn't it? How she persists in the face of nobody's interest.

How she lavishes Pond's Classic Caring Crème in grudging 3AM light, electricity hauled from the dark to service her futile salvage effort.

How she creeps into the kitchen for coffee draped in a 30-year old robe, the good one reserved for the inevitable hospital visit (as she would explain if anyone asked).

How she is out the door in her sensible shoes, immune to the street's indifference, persistent in her flaws despite being trained to please.

How as a smoother version of herself, better packaged, she was a pleasant woman, but she is no longer pleasing.

In fact she can be very unpleasant, though combed, usually, and clean, doddering along in the general rush.

How she can't even knit worth beans or imagine anyone else's misery.

Soul, how you groan, poor soul, in such company.

Mystery

The man they sent to campus once a week to parlay with those of us interested used this word often, soothing our perplexities with its soft three beats. I took it to mean *unknown*, but lately it seems to mean, *continuously being revealed*, like the deer that fill the woods in these parts.

One waited to cross the road the other day, cautious and pedestrian. Driving by, I glimpsed the glazed pools of its eyes opened wide and in the rearview mirror saw the grace of its gait, head unmoving as legs lightly plied a sure scatter of hoofs on asphalt to the other side, where it resumed its disappearance.

Cryptic

Fascination of shapes
                    that signal
what might come.

A hawk on a high limb,
                    chest an urn
waiting empty in the sun.

A key's cryptic edge
                    that exerts
owner's privilege.

To the searching eye,
                    any thing
can suggest an opening.

Abraham and Sarah Get the Unlikely News

Her husband sits in the center of the painting,
lifting a languid finger toward her.

She leans out of the house
as if to restrain herself from escape.

That's a gnarled hand, clutching the doorframe.
It's the moment after her laugh.

> *After I am waxed old shall I have pleasure,*
> *my lord being old also?*

God chooses to ask Abraham about this:

> *Why did she laugh?*

> but she's the one to answer:
> *I laughed not.*

To which the creator of the universe responds with a careless

> *Nay but thou didst laugh*
> or *Yes you did. You laughed.*

> depending on the translation.

But no matter; she lies and it doesn't make a difference
because then

> *the men rose up from thence.*

It was time to wrangle over Sodom and Gomorrah
and the issue of Lot's wife.

Of the Career of That Enigmatic Man,

nothing much to remark.

The case is closed.
It's a tale unknown,
singular as a forest
flower, unsown,
part of no garden,
of a color vague
as the maples' pink
spring haze.

Whatever transpired left
with his last breath,
and though other tongues
may take it up,
for all I know,
there's nothing to remark,
just another career
canceled in the dark.

St. Joseph's Church, Stephentown, New York

Little church fitted out in oak,
a nutshell or reversed boat,
small barque, four o'clock,
autumn dark.

He's gone again,
again he's gone
—toppled tree,
comet pulled down,

daily distress
that asks no less
than that we contrive
to bring him back alive.

Light wind frets the beams.
A warped kneeler keens.
Our silence could be prayer
or mere reverie

as we ply to renovation
from catastrophe—
rough reckoning,
wide sea.

Martin Burnham, 1959–2002

Too poor, too tough—missionaries
made bad hostages, but he kept them both.

The expensive raid could not be repeated—
besides, maintenance was easy.

At night, chaining the husband to a tree
passed for security,

and even when his ribs ridged his filthy shirt,
he could be trusted with the rice.

Though his questions were annoying, in the end,
the kidnapper himself wondered

what kind of God guided the rescuer's bullet
straight to Martin's heart.

Village Church

That bird like no bird and half a horse
hold up the doorway and march to the curve of the arch.

Someone said, *Here—St. Martin,*
and maybe a pelican to fill up the space.

Someone's hands cut and hefted
a sliver of limestone,

A mason good at birds who emerged winter nights
sooty with the brazier smoke.

Someone selected colors for the scene that would be
a village story for centuries.

Then they left on a road later paved
to bring me,

fretted by the same north wind that took the paint,
then most the rest.

Who's to tell what's left?
What was an idea

is now just a suggestion,
stone on the way back to what it came from.

The Winchester Bible

Filigree in foil, beasts
done delicately, vine
and blossom intricacy
to the glory of God,
by a king's generosity,
the first letter of each chapter
done separately.

          Though scribes
must adhere to accuracy,
illluminators may surprise
with nature transmogrified
in colors from stones
mined from shores unknown,
blues and vermillions,
tiny universes compact
and moving, as in

          Not one,
but an infinity of suns,
said Giordano Bruno
before his burning.

Wild Carrot

Here again, though last summer I shelved you in simile's warehouse (white rose window, fireworks, exploding star).

I diced and rhymed you, blended you into statements (order, wisdom, nature) and alluded to past courtiers who decked your ferny fronds in their hair.

Now you are back, simply yourself.

The mind throws up its hands and admits you are not beckoning; you have escaped metaphor's closet.

Rampant along the roads, thickest in the ditches, swaying to torrents of traffic, complacent as if waltzing, irreducible something slipped away from well-phrased praises, from history or fabrication, your perplexing beauty a signal from another imagination.

Hypocrite

The faithless mind
        that smirks, loiters,
          and cannot keep quiet

like the reverent painter
        who worked in holy poses
        but spent nights in riot,

who brooded over the solid nugget
        of nothing, swooned
        for its black-pearl-perfect

vacancy, who trolled the void
        even as he colored
        the Mater's eyes

with possibility.

Why Should We Think

*Why should we think that God's imagination
and love might be exhausted?*
—CARDINAL LEO JOSEPH SUENENS

Imagine God imagining that small, blue space in this winter sky.
A reminder from the absent sun? Mere design? An eye?

But why should God's imagination stop with clouds and trees?
Why stop there?
                                       Include ice, bitter nights,
include the news, and the beauty of views like these
becomes a side line, like the gas that emerges with crude,
a vaporous waste flamed skyward.

                              We're moved
to dwell Portia-like in the suburbs of God's imagination
while the real action's in the forum, assassination.

Jonah

He's the one who made the trip—
the ship, the whale, another three days

shouting through the city. Now this—
to miss from his perch outside the walls

the destruction he'd described so well,
circumvented by their cheap tricks

like swathing the cattle in sackcloth.

What if Jesus' Sign of Jonah was not
three days in the whale/tomb then out

but the sign of one hundred and twenty thousand
relieved Nineveans stretching arms skyward

in thanks for unmerited mercy,
the very sight of their backs

signaling a senseless peace,
a gratuitous clemency?

The commandments in shards
and the sun still over them.

Ascension Thursday

This is her gift: an amber rosary with a silver man where one
is supposed to stop and begin, to switch thoughts, a path or a chain.

I brought her lilacs, though the lawn in that place was deep in them.

She saw the joke. *You brought me lilacs—from New York?*

                                                            Her voice.

The flower stalls are filled again, profusion pressed from a hard winter,
scent and frill from once dull branches, gleam from her beads, the day a man

went up alone to the sky.

Feast of the Immaculate Conception

A dull day in December.

Dead grass shows where I passed
along the snowy path:
essence of winter smudged
back to the particular.

Frost-struck stalks line
the ruin of the lost garden.

Summer is hard to remember,
harder still to find what fits
between this world and my idea of it.

Surrounding Field

Surrounding Field

Accounts

Mother and I on the front porch, eyeing
the sun's struggle skyward. We talked stocks,
tax, bequests, the silver set—

When the sun found us,
we were off, investing effort in the day
in expectation of being repaid

by the crotchety Accountant
who'd calculate our worth according
to our use of time.

Maybe Mother would go dice green tomatoes
or pickle watermelon rinds, faded condiments
to be dabbed dutifully from jelly jars.

Now, with all that I savor,
why can't I remember those mornings
as her love's wary tender

and balance the account in her favor?

Inheritance

Cold was the principal fact and obstacle, even when sun filled the frosted windows and March shadows lay longer, a dead weight waiting on the bed to forestall the needed get up and go, lank in clothes that shrank the skin, ice in the bucket, purpled fingers. Months and months—cold, fire, and wood to saw haul split stack and then trudge back to the contingent lamp light in the one warm room.

Thus, the life of Stephen Post, my progenitor, a London carpenter, who sailed up the Connecticut River to a rocky holding near Hartford.

Thrift kept his lamp lit, thrift and craft, thin credos of parsimony and distance passed to me along with his Bible. In it, he recorded his age, his children—a creditable accumulation, property hedged cannily, with scant attention to the Bible's strange tales of generosity.

The Heathen School in Cornwall, Connecticut, 1817—1826

*Since he who is saved, behaves, pious New Englanders
founded a school for native boys to learn the bible,
stop dancing and eat at table.*

You will be sad, yes, that's Satan's test,
but pray it off, let worldly goods
be recompense for the expense
of gloom on long afternoons

and dwell upon this boon:
you're saved, your soul no more
is webbed in trees or running
wild with the waterways.

Possess yourself from death
by cutting bonds to earth. Pray alone,
and in your self-sufficiency, see
that what you thought was home

is mere scenery, benighted,
though you may have thought it,
by sun and moon and fire,
well warmed and well lighted.

Pewter

She said why talk there's God who gives me what I need He guides me and later she said some mornings I just say it's too much I can't get up and then she said it's all so hard it's been a hard life.

Her hair, her nails, well-groomed, a blue scarf, a nice-looking older lady. Lunch. The day was the color of the barrel of a gun, of pewter, stand-in for silver, our thrifty ancestors made porringers with it, spooning us its lead. There's nothing else to say, all this talk, a waste of breath, she said.

Tax Time

What though my bodie runne to dust?
—GEORGE HERBERT

It's chemistry not character I say.
He nods. We are mourning his mother

dead of cigarettes, as we do each year
while he prepares my mother's taxes.

Next, we touch on his attempts to quit.
He's a big man with fussy habits.

He highlights certain sums
and staples pages with a round

device like a torch. It's got his name on it.
Rich. *We'd be happy*

for a few weeks when she got back,
but then she'd slip. She couldn't stop.

The torch stands on its end,
ready for his big hand, each grip a perfect clip.

Maybe he and Mother had a smoke
together when she could get here herself.

We both like his character.
His lips move over a tricky transfer.

Tax Time

In ink, he makes a note next to a number
he lit in yellow. *Habits are terrible things*

I say, not meaning it, liking the way he's kept
his hair blond. His mother rests

in a quiet hill behind the Chevrolet sign.
He's a Christian of the kind

who won't burn their dead
because they wait for the Resurrection—

pure characters set free
by divine alchemy.

The Visit

He will be our guide even to the end.

My brother and his family come to visit.
His son offers me a bottle with no message in it.
Possibly ironic, he slips it back into his pocket.
I offer coffee, but they will have none of it.
Wary of my fancy habits,
they've brought instant in single packets.
I borrow their car and find Dad in it.
"You can have this when I'm finished," he says, meaning his jacket
mended in duct tape, not the new one in his closet.

"You're not finished," I lie or think I am lying.
On Delancey I realize I don't know where I'm going.
I can't complete our trip, but don't like admitting it,
and can't go back to that bunch drinking
bad coffee after leaving
the old boy in their car without an opening,
not like a soul still living.

Repair

I gave a party and everybody came, the usual disaster.
>The boy I called to fix it arrived in combat gear. Snipers swarmed the place.

Later, I remembered the party's better moments, such
>as when Aunt Chris reminded Uncle Hank how he fell in love with her when he saw her opening that big door and it seemed he did recall because he joked *Maybe they should make heavier doors.*

And my brother kissed his wife on her mouth, avoiding
>the oxygen tube, and James declared twice that it was the best ham he had ever tasted, never mind he couldn't recall which of us he married.

And who knows, maybe the kid in khakis made it back
>to tell stories about the ways he'd learned to fix what looked hopeless.

Particular

That's my self on the way out, composite that's made me,
horde of useful habits and some
attractive peculiarities.

Like a fish in the great shoal striving upstream,
I'll be mere muscle and upward strain, part of a great
reversed river, my loss, but for the bears, a gain.

Think of it, my self no more! Not that
I've been a fixed star. Nowadays, I look like
my father in the mirror.

Behind me, the usual résumés, the usual
errors, a succession of roles, reduced
now to Woman Bystander, old.

Yet who is this who ponders, and from whence
this sense that in the coming dark
there is a place particularly marked?

Love and Do What You Will
—ST. AUGUSTINE

He must mean something
by this love that I
don't know.

It could be something
like the sudden stab
I feel

looking at some things,
something like pity,
tender

tendering, somehow
moved by another
being,

the way it somehow
within its whatness
persists

even seeming, some way
to thrive. Lately, your
profile

touches me somehow;
when you're unaware
of me

and fully, some way,
yourself, in your thought
apart

and yet in some way,
in your ease, a part
of me.

I try sometimes to
speak to you of love,
but like

trees that shield, some days,
our house from sun, I
am mute.

Manna

*He gave you manna to eat
in the wilderness.*

Just to entice the moody boy,
the worried youth who would neither

marry my daughter nor go away,
I planted potatoes.

He said he'd once dug them up
and liked their unexpected heft—

beneath a dead vine, sustenance.
He wasn't used to a world that generous.

So I filled the rows.

But he brought his own blight,
dark in the mind's eye, thick

in the throat. He couldn't feed
on anything easy, couldn't

accept any
unearned cordiality.

Warmth
—TO MY GRANDCHILDREN

A man paralyzed from the neck down, home after ten
months of staring at a hospital ceiling,
said even when suffering, when there
is no language, there is warmth he said
and called this soul and seemed entitled
to his opinion—

To celebrate a martyr, the priest wore red, diaphanous,
I could tell he enjoyed its light movement. It was a bright day in late summer,
he stood on the steps after Mass still
fire-plumed—

I would like to comfort you with words like soul, with
the red-orange robe fluttering on Essex
Street, but to you they are strange

and incomprehensible, like an ancient feast I read of,
when worshippers warmed the air with
the blood of four hundred slaughtered
beasts and left only a pile of bones.

Angles of Repose

Three Saints

*. . . all the saints adore Thee, casting down their
golden crowns around the glassy sea.*
—REGINALD HEPER

From the crowd-cloud of witnesses, these
I unaccountably select, my elect—daughters blessed,

though hysterical, limited or credulous—
sometimes one, sometimes all at once.

They are casting down their golden crowns,
which the sea ingests indiscriminately,

flavoring Kateri's tears, cooling Teresa's ecstasy.
The sea grinds down all to holy particles,

reduces Lucy's gouged eyes and Teresa's
golden lance to plankton,

and stays opaque to my questioning gaze.

The Famous Ecstasy

In The Cornaro Chapel in Santa Maria della Vittoria,
Bernini carved St. Teresa about to be impaled
by a golden, flame-tipped spear
held by a winged boy.

The marble almost moves with her sighs.
Her head thrusts back. The comely youth's hand
moves toward her robe that swirls
as if it wanted to be off.

Mouth agape, eyes closed, cheeks smooth—
after years of labor toward this inmost mansion,
at forty, she's turned to Psyche,
ageless and renewed.

The eight brothers who commissioned this scene
are sculpted in stone balconies. Two look.
One reads a book. What is spiritual here?
They are clearly not at prayer.

Teresa's chest heaves beneath
her drapery. She later wrote that she
was most herself when caught in this exigency,
brimming from a center fully hers.

The winged youth stirs. Her robe's
manic fluttering shudders the air.
One confessor instructed her to laugh
when such visions appeared.

Behind her, Bernini carved and gilded lines
radiating from above the frame,
as if from an energy that his art
could not contain.

For all their imagined heat, the stone is cold.
Through distance, the story unfolds,
far from the brothers in their balconies,
far from me, left with lines
that remove rather than define.

St. Teresa Wrote

Dank air furls into the subway car
with his stink,
distinctive as the scent of cats
or the monkey house.

Passengers shrink.

Imagine such a stench,
unwashed nuns in greasy habits,
a damp refectory.

Teresa reads aloud:
*In speaking of the soul, we must
always think of it as spacious,
ample, and lofty.*

One-Sided Dialogue Concerning the Soul

Like the old friend who calls
only to tell you about herself,
the mind does all the talking.

It's so interesting.
Besides, it thinks
that the soul is not very bright.

In that place within the many mansions,
the mind doubts that the soul
would know where to hang the pictures.

The mind is almost ready to give up on the soul,
except it hears a humming somewhere,
something knitting together,

like a great tree in full leaf.

Annunciation

Some don't like the choice the scene suggests,
that Mary had the power to share her flesh.

No Leda and the Swan scene this,
but a feathery visitor in full dress,

robes unkempt with the force of descent,
coming not to sentence but to bless.

Hail. Tentative and courteous.
Because the first step had to be her yes.

Feast of the Assumption

Mid August. Nests are fledged
and the woods quiet down.

She was clothed in the sun.
Reverent angels hauled her to her throne.

Empty sack, thickened, bent,
not flesh in its flourish, but what's left.

The furrowed queen reigns.

Possible Saint

Hello she said and seemed glad, looking at me as if I were a person she had missed, and I felt that not having seen her in a while was too bad and basked in her energy outward but also thought she is not very selective, she would like the whole world to come to dinner and exclaim in that same tone of delight over the olives or whatever small offering. So she meant it though it didn't mean much and I shouldn't take her welcome personally.

There was a sheen about her, of holiness or of self-satisfaction. She had put her thoughts elsewhere, on reserve, not in the form of questions. She was genial but a little shocked that the choir sang the Gloria during Lent. I had to ask why not. Because you don't, she said. Not that she judges.

St. Lucy

Saint of the blind because she cannot see.
Saint of the dark season because her name means light.

Wreathed in candles, faces of girls in white.
She rushes outward, a pure beam,

she's the waiting fire
that arrives and arrives again,

eyes needless to mark
the obliteration of the dark

as she flames within.

Now, she's a porcelain girl with a violin.
Turn her on her pedestal to play,

her gracious light
reduced to tinny music

to keep the night at bay.

Feast of the Transfiguration, August 6

Transfiguration, Hiroshima.
Flesh into glory, flesh into ash.

Some things don't seem to exist, but the mind insists.
Some things exist, but the mind resists.

That a body alight can come back.
The mind is fatally attracted.

Eyes can see things.
People are always seeing things.

What looked like death and suffering.
Into another realm is all.

Pure light, says the commentary,
in and with God so deep he became pure light.

Iris

A chandelier flaming with candles of iris,
casting light that lit only itself, as stained glass,
afternoons full of clouds, summons light from nowhere.

Look, Mother, I said, seeking to please, but she
had disappeared from mortal eyes, cosmos
imploded to fleck, compressed in death.

Nonetheless, the candle iris flared, bodiless blue
matter surviving, promise forever arriving, grace and pardon,
flame and flower from a long-gone garden.

Vespers

... in the evening, blue,
tender yet terrible too
with the wind's weight
and I shrink with a need to hold tight,
to keep still,

as a child-drawn tree will
stand lollipop straight
in the human need to alter
what is forever off-kilter.

Crèche

When the mind stops probing,

when the mind for a moment omits judgment,

the two cheap statues—bemused couple over their child,

the standard-issue duo—form with their bodies,

with their backs' curves over the baby,

with the folds of their robes rhythmically aligned,

a circle not quite complete, a harmony of complementary curves

in which the eye, without the mind's equivocations,

in a certain light,

can discern peace.

(1)

During the Prayer of the Faithful,

I look up to the shock
of white phlox
paired with white asters.

Flecks of dim and distant stars,
lodged in temporary state,
a crystal vase.

Chips of night sky,
a still life in moon shades,
reticent drama of no color.

Like Shakespeare's *strategic opacity*—
the hero's thoughts are unknown
and color's lack is eloquent

as a vacated tomb,
white light that lingers
from the blaze of what has gone.

(2)

It's not in the light
that suffuses space
but in the seed that needs
only a moment of sun
to grow where you expected
something else to come.

Who says sky is where
since you can't be sure
this is not its place,
and you may
touch it on the way
to somewhere else.

(3)

One note or voice,
or light or angle,
or color—

Those times, I swear
that one moment
will suffice,

I claim future states
of loss acceptable,
a fair price.

(4)

Something loves
my refusal to go quietly,
dotes on the mind that debates,

lights the burning bush
off the beaten track,

and waits.

(5)

Words not my own
shapes of sound
ancestral songs
strange as any family story.

(6)

They're just wrens,
but when they stop,
how silent the landscape.

St. Kateri Tekakwitha

Orphaned and half blinded by smallpox,
the *Lily of the Mohawks*, inspired
by the missionaries to *Perpetual Virginity*.

How can I pray, how pray
to this broken child?
She can scarcely trace the way.

Future saint stinking of bear fat,
she stumbles to the mission house
along the only path left to her.

Life of the woods brought low,
she takes the trail to safety
and the glitter of a strange cup.

Piety

After the dishes, when she sat down to say the rosary,
she heard the snap in the kitchen and thought,
No more mouse. She took the bait quick.
and went on, finding safety by asking for it.

Sibilance like a thin surge over a rough beach
above the rush of trucks up First Avenue,
clink of plastic beads, clatter of consonants,
sheen of small sounds over the byways,

over the shuffling of the mouse's hungry offspring,
their vocabulary of need not much smaller
than the words she repeats, ten by ten,
battering the evening that darkens as earth heaves west.

The Rosary

Another
poor
banished
child
of Eve,
I join
Sundays
during Lent,
observer
or penitent.

    Light
    Joy
    Sorrow
    Glory
    Each day
    five stories
    around a mystery
    to think about
    while keeping
    count.

        Ten times
        the plea
        for Mary
        to pray for us
        because we
        fail to
        and must
        seek recourse
        from her,
        the source,

a welling
spring,
air,
Hopkins'
*world-
mothering*
atmosphere
that battens
down
stone.

    After ten
    to her,
    a *Glory Be*
    to the distant three
    then again
    decades that
    stop don't end
    their sound
    in the empty church
    hush hush hush.

Former Doves

*. . . the Holy Spirit descended on
him in bodily form, like a dove . . .*

The city's unloved flock
wobble thumb-shaped skulls,

ready to murmur and seethe
at any donor's feet.

To show that the lowly
can bestow, they forego

garbage cans' easy
abundance to accept

rye crumbs from old hands
with courteous coos and hums.

Some mornings,
a flock surprises,

emerging from a roof
to explode as one

glorious body in the sun.

Ritual

The field is empty because the snow
is so deep the deer don't dare go
beyond their height and so light
the least bird weight won't hold.

I come with my odd equipment
before the buried brook
carves back its curving line
and nearby pines litter the field.

At first, I sink and flail,
the landscape's only imperfection,
until a step becomes a glide,
the deep lifts me, and I move.

I'm most alive yet not myself,
only breath and hiss of skis.
This hour is a crystal cut from time,
or a polar ocean slowed in cold.

Ice may be how water is most itself,
as I in these strange movements find myself,
as the dried grass rising along the road
remembers in movement how to unfold.

The Apple Tree

Why in that lot on Houston Street, in a far corner,
as if forced back by the bottles launched at it,
does an apple tree bud in the killing cold?

February was balmy and early March warmed the ground.
Street trees held their fire, but the apple
was urgent to flower once more.

I wish it had delayed, but it was tricked
by what we've done to weather,
and now blooms too soon, betrayed.

Shadrach, Meshach, and Abednego

*. . . and Nebuchadnezzar said to them, "Is it true,
Shadrach, Meshach and Abednego,
that you do not serve my gods?"*

Summer was sluggish, slow
and thick, but this dénouement
is operatic—

seared by frost flames,
trees stretch their arms
for my astonishment.

Here's the fiery furnace, and the only way
out is through. Here's the gold
those three wouldn't worship

Or their glorious walk through the fire—
vision or admonition, God's garment
of light or death's flaming agent.

There's a reckless air to this leaving.
I wonder what will guide me
through such burning.

Forecast

He who seeks his strength in flesh will inhabit this,
Jeremiah said, referring to the desert, and flung down a jug.

Terra cotta shards flecked the valley floor.
The crowd gawked.

Trust in the Lord and fear no heat,
Jeremiah said. It was the era of orderly weather.

It was back in the day
when the desert stayed put.

Disturbances were the result of failures
to communicate, and the sun's coming

and going marked progress
toward an event that the authorities

kept announcing and postponing, but,
it was understood, they could control.

He makes his wind blow and the waters flow

Thus Psalm one forty seven, verse eighteen.

If the Book is Divine Emanation, open
to Cabbalists, God's composite Name

waiting to be seen, a code to crack,
what might this number mean?

Line nine: *He gives the animals their food
and to the young ravens* when they cry.

He's also busy in the sky, naming stars
and sending *snow like wool* in line ten.

But why then

strange warmth this March morning
radio voice foretelling

an unseasonable storm
from energies unknown?

Clouds lower over the East River
and a briny tide slides uptown.

Faith

*Only by living completely in the world
does one learn to have faith.*
—DIETRICH BONHOEFFER

In the park after our inconclusive talk—
what words for the oak? Pure bounty,
beauty, uplift,

stout heart? What force can reach that loft—
pith grown from sun and rain
and rock sift?

Spread double the reach of its branches,
roots riddle its plot, tendrils assembled
through and out

that mass to form an anchor, counterweight,
power more great
than thought.

Let all the trees of the forest sing for joy

Centuries, and not a day gone by that somewhere a mind
    has not touched the psalmist's singing trees,
    the fields and mountains shouting for joy—

has not touched and pondered what the writer fabricated
    from the few forests in dusty Palestine and
    passed down.

Over and over scribes transmitted it, in small square letters, with ivory or gold or silver pens, avoiding
    any alloy used in war—

scribes and choruses echoed the moment when the
    writer was not deaf to the singing of the trees.

Sequoias as old as the psalm breathe yet in thunderous
    quiet, fashion themselves from weather and
    unfurl a canopy tentatively,

tentative as the reader's mind that touches the psalm and
    reaches skyward toward the edge of vision.

So, My Saints

For all Thy saints, who from their labors rest,
Who Thee by faith before the world confessed.
    —WILLIAM WALSHAM HOW

So, my saints, you three are at rest,
wherever you are, you labor no more,
your measure has been allotted and you join the throng
that Bishop How celebrated in song.

I too would like to set you to a tune, tune you up,
march you along, but your stories don't compute,
a line won't form, you make your ways alone,
trailing peculiarities vexing as my own.

In a statue of Mary at the Met, Hall of Medieval Art,
she's a lithe girl with strong hands, trunk propped
to bear the child up. He reaches toward her cheek,
a touch she smiles to accept.

Carved from oak, a slight girl like a young tree
whose gaze says, *God reached into himself and created me*

and all of us, my saints, all singularities.

Notes

"*Why My Soul, are you downcast?*" Psalm 42:5

"Abraham and Sarah Get the Unlikely News" Genesis 18:12-15

"Why Should We Think" epigraph from Cardinal Suenens December, 2014 *Living with Christ* New London, CT: Bayard Inc.

"Ascension Thursday" The fortieth day after Easter Sunday, commemorating the Ascension of Christ into heaven, according to Mark 16:19, Luke 24:51, and Acts 1:2 Catholic Encyclopedia http://www.newadvent.org/cathen/a.htm

"Feast of the Immaculate Conception" In the Constitution Ineffabilis Deus of 8 December, 1854, Pius IX pronounced and defined that the Blessed Virgin Mary '... was preserved exempt from all stain of original sin.' Catholic Encyclopedia http://www.newadvent.org/cathen/a.htm

"The Visit" Psalm 48:14

"St. Teresa Wrote" *Interior Castle* page 37 translated by E. Allison Peers. Garden City, New York: Image, 1961.

"Manna" Deuteronomy 8:15.17

"Annunciation" In the sixth month after the conception of St. John the Baptist by Elizabeth, the angel Gabriel was sent from God to the Virgin Mary to tell her she was to give birth to Jesus. Luke 1:26.38 http://www.newadvent.org/cathen/a.htm

"Feast of the Transfiguration, August 6" This feast is observed on August 6 to commemorate the manifestation of the Divine glory recorded by St. Matthew (Chapter 17) http://www.newadvent.org/cathen/a.htm

Notes

"Feast of the Assumption" Regarding the day, year, and manner of Our Lady's death, nothing certain is known. Catholic faith, however, has always derived our knowledge of the mystery from Apostolic Tradition. http://www.newadvent.org/cathen/a.htm

"Former Doves" Luke 3:22

"Shadrach, Meshach and Abednego" Daniel 3:14

"Let all the trees of the forest sing for joy" Psalm 96: 12

"So, My Saints" italicized lines from Meister Eckhart August, 2014 *Living with Christ* New London, CT: Bayard Inc.

www.ingramcontent.com/pod-product-compliance
Lightning Source LLC
Chambersburg PA
CBHW051704090426

42736CB00013B/2538